Original title:
The Jellyfish's Journey

Copyright © 2025 Creative Arts Management OÜ
All rights reserved.

Author: Julian Carmichael
ISBN HARDBACK: 978-1-80587-298-6
ISBN PAPERBACK: 978-1-80587-768-4

A Ballet of Color

In the ocean's grand stage,
A dance of weird grace,
With tentacles flailing,
In a colorful race.

They twirl in delight,
With whimsy in sight,
A jelly ballets,
In day and in night.

Their costumes so bright,
Occasionally swish,
When they tickle fishies,
In a jelly-ish wish.

The audience giggles,
At each silly flail,
A spectacle shines,
In this watery trail.

Fluidity in Stillness

Drifting through waters,
With a bob and a sway,
A jelly so zen,
In its own special way.

No rush or a hurry,
In its slow-motion flight,
It preens like a diva,
In the shimmering light.

As fish dart and dart,
With quickness, they tease,
This jelly just floats,
Like it owns the high seas.

A stillness amusing,
In a world full of spin,
The jelly keeps chill,
With its goofy wild grin.

Refracted Light

Through the waves it glimmers,
A disco ball splash,
Each ray bends and breaks,
Like a painter's wild splash.

Sunlight gets playful,
In ripples and waves,
Painting jellies in colors,
Like quirky knave braves.

The way it reflects,
Is a source of pure glee,
If laughter could sparkle,
It would dance in the sea.

With each twinkle and wink,
It fancies the day,
The jelly can't help
But put on a display.

The Soft Dance of Nature

In the sea's gentle arms,
A jig it performs,
A wobbly ballet,
With no need for norms.

With a swoosh and a swish,
It glides through the blue,
Each movement a tickle,
Just what jellyfish do.

It floats in a whirl,
In a jelly-like trance,
A soft, silly waltz,
If the sea gives a chance.

The oceans all giggle,
At this splashy delight,
For in the deep waters,
Nothing feels quite right.

A Mysterious Pilgrim

In the ocean blue, a wanderer does rap,
With tentacles waving, not a map in his flap.
He bumps into fish, they giggle and dart,
"Who needs direction when you have heart?"

Through coral lanes, with a silly pose,
He dances along where the seaweed grows.
A bubble pops loud, he jumps with a fright,
"Oh well," he decides, "this is pure delight!"

Friends wave and tease, a slapstick ballet,
This odd little ghoul makes joy in the bay.
With a twirl and a swirl, he claims the best view,
In the laughter of currents, he finds something new.

Currents of Serenity

Bobbing along, like a goofy balloon,
Each wave is a giggle, each tide is a tune.
A flip here and there, oh what fun to be found,
With glee in the water, he spins round and round.

The sun beams down, a spotlight of joy,
He's not just a creature, he's a playful buoy.
With a whirl and a twirl, he entertains schools,
While drifting through waters, his dance breaks the rules.

Gliding with grace, it's a festival scene,
The jelly-like jester, a hilarious dream.
In the currents of calm, where laughter does swell,
He revels in tides, oh do tell! Do tell!

Veils of Light

With sparkling tendrils, he paints in the sea,
A canvas of bubbles, what a sight to see!
He twinkles like stars in a watery dance,
Floating carefree, never missing a chance.

As he drifts through the beams, a glow on his face,
He whispers to shells, "Isn't life a nice place?"
With hoots from the lobsters and snickers from crabs,
He giggles in colors, what a delightful drab!

A tapestry woven with humor in fins,
Among the bright corals, where laughter begins.
In veils of pure light, this traveler beams bright,
As the waves play along in the soft, salty night.

The Rhythm of the Deep

In the deep, the dance floor is set every night,
With bubbles as beats and disco fish bright.
He shimmies on sand, with laughter in tow,
A rhythmic adventure, what a charming show!

With each little jig, he astonishes shrimp,
They wiggle and giggle, this nautical blimp.
With a jolt and a bounce, he spins on the spot,
The undersea party, he's quite the hot shot!

The seaweed sways along, to music unseen,
With a splash and a dash, the fun is routine.
In the rhythm of waves, he's the king of the sweep,
A jester in currents, in the heart of the deep!

The Ocean's Ballet

In the depths where the weird things glide,
A dancer swirls with no need to hide.
With bells on their tentacles, they twirl,
Leaving fish in giggles and a whirl.

They bump into coral, a clumsy fate,
Saying, "Excuse me!" while they contemplate.
With a wobbly grace, they entertain,
Creating laughter like ocean rain.

Oh, see how they float with such flair!
Like floaty umbrellas without a care.
Bobbing and weaving, what a sight!
Making waves of fun both day and night.

In the vast blue, a circus unfolds,
With jelly acrobats leading the bold.
They brighten the sea, spreading joy,
Crowning the currents, life's buoyant toy.

Echoes of the Abyss

Down where the seaweed whispers low,
A jelly winks as it steals the show.
With a bounce in its pulse and a giggle so sweet,
It spins through the currents, a dance on repeat.

The crabs start to clap, they're quite the fans,
While sharks flash their grins and offer their hands.
The deep has a rhythm, a kooky sound,
As jellies jive, twirling round and round.

In caverns of darkness, the laughter grows,
As creatures unite for the jellyfish shows.
Bubbles rise up in a frothy cheer,
"What a wacky jelly!" echoes far and near.

So join in the fun, drift where they sway,
For under the waves, it's a jolly display.
With giggles and wiggles, they shine like bright stars,
The remix of nature, and here come the bazaar!

Sea's Serene Traveler

Beneath the waves, where the sunlight fades,
A mellow mover in vibrant cascades.
Drifting along, with no cares on its mind,
A peaceful performer, one of a kind.

It floats through the reefs, on a lazy ride,
Bumpin' and crashin', it laughs with pride.
"Oops, pardon me!" it softly declares,
As fish blink in shock from its wild flares.

With a whimsical swish and a floaty groove,
It scoots past shells with a soft, gentle move.
In the backdrop of water, a comic endeavor,
In serene, silly ballet, they float forever.

So here in the sea, without worry or haste,
Jelly's escapades are never a waste.
With giggles and bubbles, they float through the day,
A soft, silly legend in their watery ballet!

Floating in the Blue

In the middle of nowhere, where the fish do play,
   A jelly floats by in a whimsical way.
With a flip and a flop, it's a sight to behold,
   An underwater droplet spun tales of old.

It wiggles and jiggles, tracing a line,
As sea creatures chuckle, saying, "Oh, that's divine!"
They mock and they tease as it bounces around,
   A jellyfish jester, in laughter entwined.

With currents to ride and bubbles to pop,
   It dances in circles, never a stop.
Cheering the waves, making all who see grin,
   Turning the ocean into a fun-filled spin.

So if you should venture where waters are clear,
Look for the jelly that's bringing good cheer.
With laughter and wobbles, it'll steal the show,
In the big turquoise world, where silliness flows!

Drifting with the Currents

Floating on a blob of goo,
With wobbly grace, it drifts anew.
A real-life pillow in the sea,
Who needs a boat? Just glide with glee.

Tangled up in dancing weeds,
A tangled mess, fulfilling needs.
Tickled by the fish so small,
In this grand ball, it'll have a ball.

Bobbing 'round like a quirky ghost,
Unbothered, it sways while it boasts.
Living life like a carefree kite,
Who knew the sea could be this light?

Sunshine gleams on its jelly skin,
It does the twist, the twirl, the spin.
A jelly party, oh what a sight,
In ocean fun, it's pure delight!

Whispers of the Ocean's Veil

In the deep, a secret chat,
Between a crab and a curious splat.
Whispers travel through the waves,
Like rumors formed in bubbly caves.

Hey there, friend, on your jelly ride,
Careful not to take a tide slide!
With a flip and a float, oh what a scene,
Laughs echo in the marine cuisine.

Octopuses share their fishy tales,
While the seaweed dances, sways, and flails.
The ocean's joke is a giggle trap,
Where jelly mess finds a cozy nap.

Underneath with bubbly flair,
Even the starfish stop and stare.
The waves are wild, full of jest,
In this funny world, we are blessed!

Dance of the Celestial Drifter

With a jiggle and a jazz-like flair,
It spins through waters without a care.
Stars above blink in surprise,
At this odd creature in the waves that flies.

Swaying to the currents' beat,
A jiggly dance, oh so sweet.
Whirling round like it's out of style,
Making waves with a spongy smile.

Fish peek out to gawk and stare,
"Is it a dancer, or just air?"
In moonlit sparkles of the night,
It plays tag with the beams of light.

Floating free, in a cosmic trance,
A jelly's life—a curious dance.
With bubbles of laughter all around,
Joy in the ocean, the best found!

Beneath the Waves of Serenity

In a peaceful dance, it floats and flops,
Through rippling blues, it gently hops.
Serene yet silly, a calming view,
It twirls with grace, in the ocean blue.

Laughter bubbles from the sea floor,
As fish giggle, and eels explore.
A jolly jelly, in its fancy dress,
Waves hello, in joyous mess.

Feeling the current, a gentle pull,
A wavy romp, delightful and full.
Playing tag with a passing whale,
In underwater fun, it'll never fail.

As sunlight filters through the tide,
It beams with joy, nothing to hide.
In a whimsical world, it finds its peace,
Beneath the waves, the giggles never cease!

An Ocean's Whisper

In the blue, where sea meets sky,
A wobbly traveler floats on by.
With tentacles like noodle strings,
A dance that's sure to make you sing.

Bumping into fish with quite a flair,
They giggle and wiggle without a care.
"Who's this blob with a silly style?"
"Just passing through, stay awhile!"

A wink, a sway, a shimmering laugh,
In salty waters, crafting its path.
No need to rush, just glide and sway,
This jiggly friend loves to play.

An ocean's whisper, full of delight,
Follows the tides both day and night.
As bubbles pop in a joyful spree,
The jester of currents, wild and free.

Translucent Pilgrimage

A clear balloon in a deep blue race,
With no destination, just a happy face.
Tentacles trailing like ribbons in air,
Wobbling along without a care.

Riding a wave on a frothy glide,
Being mistaken for a piece of tide.
"Hey there, buddy, are you lost too?"
"Nope, just floating, how 'bout you?"

Creatures wave as they pass on by,
A soft hello, a friendly pie.
Sayingfish tales that make stories swell,
In the great blue, all is well.

Belly up to the surface, just for fun,
Soak in the rays, till the day is done.
A pilgrim of light on an endless spree,
Floating and giggling, forever carefree.

Journey Beyond the Shore

Drifting beyond the sandy stretch,
Where sunbeams and seaweed seem to etch.
A soft jelly glides, with no set plan,
With wiggles and giggles, it's quite the fan.

It bumps into clams that clack and chatter,
"Look at that blob! Does it really matter?"
"Impressive, isn't it? Such fancy moves!"
With a squish and a splash, it grooves and grooves.

Navigating reefs, a curious soul,
Chasing pretty fish while taking a stroll.
Through bubbles and giggles, it sails with glee,
A comical sight in the vast, deep sea.

Champagne of the ocean, so light and free,
With every little bob, it shares its spree.
An odyssey filled with laughter and cheer,
Who knew the best journeys were floating near?

Awakening in the Deep

In the depths, where creatures sleep,
A giggly wanderer takes a leap.
With a bounce and a wiggle, it's all in the fun,
Who knew the ocean could be this run?

A wink at the shrimp, a nod to the crab,
A friend to all, bright, round, and fab.
"Come join the party! It's quite a scene!"
With echoes of laughter, the ocean's a dream.

Float past the corals, a wiggly show,
Where the antics of sea life steal the flow.
With every new tide, a fresh little spin,
Awakening glee from the deep within.

So dance with the waves, in this vibrant blue,
Where jelly and laughter become part of the crew.
An awakening joy, an aquatic jest,
In the salty embrace, we are truly blessed.

Embracing the Flow

In a wiggle and a sway,
The sea is my ballet.
With tentacles that dance,
I'm in a foam-filled trance.

I float with grace, oh me!
What's this snare? A cup of tea?
Doubled over in a whirl,
Who knew I'd be a swirling girl?

I've dodged a crab's quick pinch,
But oh, these barnacles, they clench!
With every tide I ride,
Under waves, I'll never hide.

On jelly wings, I fly free,
Home is where the jelly be!
A giggle floats upon the sea,
I'm the queen of jelly glee!

Echoes of an Ancient Sea

Bouncing in a salty spree,
Echoes call from depths of glee.
Ancient tales float on the breeze,
I think I'll join the seaweed tease.

With a wiggle and a jig,
I might just be the sea's own pig!
Who needs a land-bound show?
When you glow, you steal the show!

The dolphins laugh as I squirt,
A burst of ink? My secret flirt!
In the deep, I am the star,
Just hope they don't take me too far!

With every loop and every twirl,
The ocean gives a giddy whirl.
Echoes of my jolly cheer,
In the waves, I shed a tear.

Gliding Through H2O

Gliding through the ocean's flow,
I'm a jelly superstar, you know!
With a bob and a swoosh, I dash,
In this vast pool, I make a splash.

Here comes a fish, with a sidelong glance,
Not quite ready for this jelly dance.
I giggle as I gently glide,
With a friendly wave, not a single slide.

Sometimes I swirl with giddy glee,
Playing tag with seaweed, whee!
Crabs scuttle, trying to catch up,
But I'm too quick—sipping from my cup!

In my watery world, laughter reigns,
With sunbeams sparkling like champagne.
Oh, the fun that we can find,
When a jelly's fate is beautifully twined.

Undersea Reverie

In the depths, I dream and play,
Bubbling thoughts float away.
A sea turtle comes to say hi,
We exchange glances; he's quite shy.

A treasure chest full of clams,
I'm not interested in their jams.
Instead, I twirl past rocks and corals,
Turning the floor into my morals.

I've nibbled on flakes from a ship's hull,
Danced with narwhals, feeling dull!
"Join me!" I shout with a jelly cheer,
"Life is a party, come lend your ear!"

Undersea friends make me beam,
Living life like a glossy dream.
With laughter floating in the blue,
A jelly's life is fun, who knew?

Wandering Among Shadows

In the moonlight, it glides with grace,
Its tentacles waving in a silly race.
With a flip and a flop, it takes to the air,
"Look at me! I'm a dance diva, beware!"

Dodging fish who swim with a frown,
"Don't you know? I'm the talk of the town!"
It juggles some bubbles and lets out a cheer,
"Watch me, world, for the comedy's here!"

Songs of the Deep Sea

In the murky depths, it sings a tune,
A catchy refrain beneath the moon.
With a wobble and wiggle, it steals the show,
Even the shy crabs can't help but glow.

"Hey there, fish! Come join my crew,
We'll throw a party, just me and you!"
Tickling the seaweed, it spins round and round,
Creating a whirlpool of laughter profound.

Silk and Seafoam

A silky sensation floats through the tide,
While seafoam giggles, it takes a ride.
"Catch me if you can!" it quips with glee,
"Life's just a wave, come dance with me!"

With bubbles for friends and tides as a stage,
It performs for the shrimp, earning applause and rage.
"Make way, make way! Here comes the flair,
A drifter of dreams in this watery air!"

Luminous Pathways

Glowing with laughter, it lights up the night,
In a sea full of giggles, it feels so right.
"Who needs a lantern? I'm bright as a star!
Just follow my glow, I promise it's bizarre!"

With flicks and flutters, it draws a bright line,
"Keep up, my friends, it's cosmic divine!"
It twists and it twirls, a glowworm in style,
The ocean can't help but giggle a while.

Timeless Tides

In a world where currents sway,
A jiggly blob swims every day.
With tentacles spreading wide,
It dances with the ocean's tide.

Bouncing off a friendly whale,
It giggles, leaving quite the trail.
Together, they whirl and dive,
In a sea where laughter's alive.

The fish all stop and stare,
As it floats without a care.
A party in the briny blue,
In every wave, it finds a cue.

Under moonlight's silver glow,
The jelly floats, enjoying the show.
With each wave a boisterous cheer,
In the tides, it's the star so clear.

A Veiled Odyssey

With a wiggle and a swirl, it glides,
In this grand aquatic ride.
Wearing nature's finest veil,
It swoops and swooshes without fail.

A crab shivers, stops to stare,
As our hero darts through the air.
In a dance that's both bold and quirky,
It's really quite the underwater turkey.

Octopuses laugh, they can't resist,
As it flips around with a little twist.
No worries in the deep blue sea,
Just jelly laughs, wild and free.

Through kelp forests, it prances bright,
Sharing joy with the fish at night.
Its journey, not one to miss,
A sea adventure filled with bliss!

The Light Beneath the Waves

Beneath the waves, a glimmer glows,
A jellyfish strikes a pose, it shows.
With flashes of colors, it's a sight,
An underwater disco, oh what a fright!

Fish stop by for the funky beat,
As it shimmies and shakes with humbling heat.
Slippery friends join the themed bash,
In the sea, there's no need to dash.

Each loop and twist is a comedy act,
With jelly antics, there's never a lack.
A swirling party, oh so spry,
Making waves as it floats on by.

It twirls through currents, a fluid dance,
Filling the ocean with its charmed prance.
With every ripple, a laughter swell,
An oddball in the ocean's carousel.

Tidal Reverie

In calm waters, where dreams collide,
A jelly dreams of a wild ride.
It bounces on the cresting foam,
Exploring beneath the salty dome.

Sandy shores, a curious crowd,
Laughing fish, they're all so loud.
With each splash, a sprinkle of glee,
As it wobbles through the sea so free.

A seagull spies and screeches loud,
"Look at that silly jelly, oh wow!"
With tendrils waving like a flag,
Each wave a laugh, not a drag.

Under the sun, it catches light,
Glistening brightly, quite the sight.
In a world full of giggles and jests,
The jelly leads, never rests!

Pulses in the Midnight Blue

In the dark, they bob and sway,
A jiggly dance, come join the play.
Floating high, they're quite the sight,
With their ghostly glow, they light the night.

Bouncing off the ocean ground,
A squishy party, laughter found.
Tentacles tickle, whoops and whirls,
Making waves with flappy swirls.

Drifting past a sleepy seal,
Silly faces, what a deal!
With a flip, they spin in glee,
Underwater antics, oh so free!

As midnight sharks let out a chuckle,
These jellies serve a giggly buckle.
In the blue, they swirl around,
Sharing secrets they have found.

Elysium Beneath the Swell

Beneath the tide, where giggles bloom,
Jellies drift with cheeky zoom.
Wobbling here and wiggling there,
With squishy joy, they float with flair.

In a cloak of starlit shine,
They wriggle through the sea, oh so fine.
With a twist, they play peek-a-boo,
Each ripple sings a silly tune.

Beneath the waves, they jest and grin,
A party where the fun begins.
Swirling tales of ocean lore,
These funny blobs get the crowd to roar!

Whispers of seaweed curl and twine,
As jellies frolic, feeling divine.
No need for shoes, they glide along,
Singing their very own silly song.

Dances with the Moonlit Momentum

In the glow of the moonlight's beam,
Jellies frolic, living the dream.
Twisting, twirling, they find their groove,
With a jellyfish jig that makes you move!

Flapping caps and swaying arms,
Creating laughter with their charms.
Floating on a wave like a clown,
With every wiggle, they won't drown!

An octopus joins, with a dance of flair,
Together they swirl, a quirky pair.
Underwater ballet, a slippery race,
With a giddy giggle, they conquer space!

Between the currents, the mischief brews,
As briny bubbles bring the blues.
With a splash and a pop, they steal the show,
In moonlit fun, they steal the flow!

Ephemeral Existence in Liquid Realms

Life's a blur beneath the sea,
Jellies drift, wild and free.
Not a care as they float about,
Spreading joy, there's no doubt!

With a wiggle and a giggle, they swirl,
Each movement sets the ocean a-twirl.
Tentacles flailing like flags of cheer,
Under the waves, they persevere.

Who knew life could be a grand jest?
Jellies swim with sheer zest!
SpongeBob laughs at their silly plight,
As they tumble in the shimmering light.

Every bounce a comedic treat,
In liquid realms, they dance on repeat.
With a wink and a flick, they make a splash,
In a world of silliness, they make a dash!

The Rhythm of Life in a Shifting Sea

A bobbing dance, all wobbly and wide,
With tentacles flapping, they sway and glide.
No worries of doom, just floating along,
A jelly ballet, they can't be wrong.

A wink and a jig, they twist in delight,
Stealing the show, without a true fight.
They shimmer in colors, a sight to behold,
As laughter erupts, their antics unfold.

In a world full of fish, they take the lead,
With slapstick charm, they fulfill every need.
The partners of humor in oceanic fun,
Beneath waves, the giggles have just begun.

So raise a fin to the jests of the tide,
With friends all around, they take it in stride.
Life in the blue, a whimsical spree,
The rhythm of life flows, wild and free.

A Celestial Voyage through Salted Waters.

Floating like stars in a watery sky,
These creatures of wonder just drift and sigh.
With glee they encounter a playful crab,
Who nips at their ghosts, oh what a jab!

A wink to a clam, they giggle and tease,
A bubble of laughter floats on the breeze.
Through salty expanses, they twirl with grace,
As humor unfurls in this vast, silly space.

With the tides as their guide, they leap and they flop,
Making waves at the surface, then on they hop.
A quest for good jokes on this aquatic trip,
With jokes made of seaweed, a punchline to rip.

The sunbeams applaud their comedic charade,
For under the waves, fun is the trade.
With each little jiggle, the ocean will sing,
A celestial dance in the splash of spring.

Drifting Through Liquid Dreams

In a dream that's liquid, they drift with glee,
A carnival ride through the salty spree.
With wobbly spins, their bodies collide,
Making jokes with the fish, their laughter's the tide.

Oh, to glide like a cloud with a silly sway,
As bubbles pop up, they're here to play.
In vivid blue depths, they twirl in a jig,
While nearby a dolphin snorts, what a big gig!

Through the kelp they meander, a whimsical maze,
Adding a punchline to the watery haze.
Not a care in the world, just fun to be had,
Even crabs at their side aren't ever too mad.

The laughter of currents, it tickles the gills,
As jellyfish joke 'neath the ocean's own thrills.
In dreams made of jelly, they float and they beam,
Creating a ruckus in blue liquid dreams.

Beneath the Waves

In the depths below where the sea creatures glide,
A jester or two drifts in joy, side by side.
With swirls and with bounces, they wiggle with flair,
A performance so funny, it's worse than a scare!

A splash and a flip, oh what a grand sight,
These masters of comedy dazzle the night.
With phosphorescent blooms lighting pathways anew,
They tickle the fancies of all who swim through.

With laughter like bubbles that tickle the nose,
They dance on the currents, like nobody knows.
A party of jollies with friends in the brine,
They sip on the currents, as if sipping wine.

So here's to the sea, where the humor runneth,
In witty embraces, the giggles are spun.
At the depths of the ocean, together they play,
In the embrace of the laughter, they drift and they sway.

Pathways of a Gelatinous Dream

In the depths where wobblers dwell,
A jiggly dance, oh what a spell!
Tentacles flail in graceful loops,
Making friends with all the fishy groups.

They glide and slide like wiggly stars,
A comedy show beneath the bars.
With each puff, they float so free,
Creating laughter in the sea.

A moonlit soup where giggles roam,
Every wave feels like a home.
With bubbles bursting, tiny sprays,
Who knew the ocean had such plays?

So let's toast with shimmering brine,
To wobbly wonders, so divine!
In every splash, a joyful scream,
The world's a stage, a jelly dream.

The Silent Ballet of the Abyss

In murky waters, shadows swirl,
A silent show that makes you twirl.
With twinkling lights they take their flight,
A shimmering dance in the deep of night.

They bounce and bob, a clumsy lot,
In pirouettes, they give it a shot.
With jelly legs and swaying grace,
Oh, what a curious spectacle in space!

As bubbles burst, they start to yawn,
A wobbly crew, till the break of dawn.
Each movement's like a playful tease,
An undersea party, if you please!

So giggle with the fishes near,
At the ballet of the briny sphere.
In laughter's waltz, we all delight,
In the silent dance of the ocean's night.

Embraced by Ocean's Breaths

Swirls of water, soft and blue,
Gentle tides, a funny crew.
They bounce along, with jelly flair,
Wobbling wildly without a care.

With every wave, they giggle loud,
Bouncing proudly, oh so proud!
They twist and turn like silly dreams,
Creating joy in two-day streams.

From coral trees to sandy beds,
They float about, no worries, no dreads.
In merry tunes of bubbles' pop,
The giggles rise, they never stop!

So raise a glass to ocean glee,
To jelly friends and their sea spree.
In laughter's tide, we're all embraced,
By waves of mirth, perfectly placed.

Bioluminescent Heartbeats

Glowing wares in ocean's night,
A flicker here, a spark so bright.
Wobbling dreams with glimmery signs,
Who knew the sea had such fun designs?

They flash like lights in crazy shows,
Jiggling lightly, where humor flows.
With every pulse, a chuckle spills,
The ocean's giggle that always thrills.

A dance of neon in the dark,
Wobbling wonders leave their mark.
In every swirl, a giggle floats,
Through depths of joy, where laughter boats.

So here's to beats beneath the waves,
To jelly friends and their funny braves.
In glowing laughs and silly slips,
We celebrate the ocean's quips.

A Choreography of Waves

In blue ballet, they twirl and sway,
With tentacles dancing, come what may.
A wobbly waltz in the salty brew,
Silly creatures in a watery zoo.

They glide in circles, quite out of sync,
With jelly-like grace, you'd laugh, you'd blink.
Round and round, they swirl and spin,
In the ocean's stage, they always win.

A flip and a flop, they do a twist,
As fish swim by and give a fist.
Quirky moves in the sun's great glow,
Jelly acrobats, putting on a show.

With bubbles galore, they frolic free,
Life's a splash, oh, can't you see?
In currents' rhythm, they're quite absurd,
Laughing under waves, not a word heard.

Celestial Driftwood

Drifting along like space debris,
Floating wood in a cosmic spree.
With stars in their bells and dreams in tow,
They glide through the depths with a graceful flow.

Astro jelly in a galactic ballet,
Hitching a ride on the Milky Way.
They wave to the fish, 'We come in peace!'
While giggling softly, 'Let's never cease!'

They float on a tide not of this Earth,
Making waves with a giggly mirth.
In the ocean's theater, they steal the scene,
With cosmic flips that are simply keen.

Under a moon of royal blue,
They sip on the sea, as jellyfish do.
Wink at the stars, they shout, "What a sight!"
Celestial drifters, dancing all night!

Beneath the Surface

Under the waves, a laughter spills,
As jelly clowns perform their thrills.
With wobbly bodies and silly grins,
They juggle plankton and race the fins.

Tickling the seaweed, throwing a jest,
Waving hello to the curious crest.
A ticklish ride on a briny tide,
In a bubbly world where giggles abide.

They bashfully blush with a pinkish glow,
As bubbles burst with a comedic show.
Underwater antics, quite the affair,
As they flail and stumble without a care.

Their tentacles wave like confetti in air,
Creating a ruckus, but who wouldn't dare?
Beneath the surface, a secret delight,
Where laughter bubbles, and joy takes flight!

Infinite Horizons

Beyond the shores, where waves collide,
Jelly mischief takes a joyous ride.
They chase the sun with a playful cheer,
To horizons infinite, far and near.

In a world of jelly, nothing amiss,
Spinning through currents, they twist and kiss.
A carnival float in a bright parade,
With looping motions, they've truly made.

On sandy stages, they mime with glee,
As toucans groan, 'What a sight to see!'
With a splash and a giggle, they frolic around,
Creating a joy that knows no bound.

Infinite horizons beckon them true,
Daring each wave to learn something new.
Their laughter echoes over the seas,
As they chase adventure with playful ease!

Beneath the Surface

In the blue, she floats with flair,
Wobbling like jelly, without a care.
Through kelp forests, she does glide,
With a grin on her face, oh what a ride!

Fish stop and stare, make a fuss,
'What's that blob? Is it one of us?'
She jiggles and wiggles, makes quite the scene,
A wobbly wonder, bright and serene.

Her tentacles wave like ribbons in flight,
Dancing around, what a silly sight!
Sharing secrets with crabby old pals,
While seahorses giggle, doing their pals.

Beneath the waves, she's the queen of fun,
In her gelatinous world, life's never done.
With a flip and a flap, she spins like a top,
Oh jelly, oh jelly, please don't stop!

a Journey Unseen

Off she goes, on a frothy spree,
Riding the current, so wild and free.
A blob of giggles, with a squishy gait,
In her ocean, who can relate?

Watch out, here comes a shellfish parade,
They shuffle along, unfazed and unafraid.
She sneezes a bubble, they scatter in shock,
'Who invited the jiggly polka-dot rock?'

Through the reefs, she wiggles and shines,
Her laughter echoes, in twisty designs.
With every swirl, sapient fish cheer,
'Here comes our jelly, bring on the beer!'

No map in hand, just smiles and glee,
In this world of water, she's truly free.
Oh, what adventures beneath the sea,
As she dances along, life's silly jubilee!

Secrets of the Deep's Gentle Traveler

A traveler floats in her silky home,
With secrets to tell, where no fish dare roam.
Her body glows softly in waves' gentle lap,
Tickling the sea urchin, giving him a clap.

As she glides past, the dolphin sways,
'What's that, a blob? Or your new way of praise?'
She spins in delight, throwing laughter their way,
'I'm just bein' me, let's play and sway!'

Corals chuckle as she drifts by,
With a wink of a wave, she says, 'Oh hi!'
Carried by currents and a pinch of good cheer,
In a world full of wonder, where's the fear?

Under the sea, where oddities rise,
She twirls through the marine life's grand surprise.
With a splash and a giggle, what a sight to behold,
A gentle traveler with stories untold!

A Dance with Neptune's Children

Neptune's children spin and twirl,
Around the jelly, giving a whirl.
'Come join the fun,' they cheer with delight,
As she jiggles along, what a joyful sight!

Crabs in tuxedos, fish in their best,
Gather together, it's a fancy fest.
Jelly, the star, with a shimmer and giggle,
Is waltzing through waves with a silly wiggle.

With each tendril bounce, a giggle's released,
'Is it a dance or just jelly-shaped beast?'
Neptune himself, with a chuckle and clap,
Joins in the jig, oh, what a mishap!

In this watery ballroom, wild and free,
They dance to the rhythm of gurgles and glee.
Jelly shines bright, in this oceanic play,
With Neptune's children, she's here to stay!

The Sea's Celestial Drifter

Drifting along in a sea of delight,
Bouncing through bubbles, a shimmering sight.
She giggles and glitters, a star in the deep,
Where turtles and dolphins learn to leap.

With each gentle pulse, she tickles the tide,
A celestial drifter, in the ocean she hides.
'What are you doing?' the octopus grins,
'Just floating along and collecting some wins!'

Through seaweed jungles, she flits like a breeze,
Sending fish into spins with the greatest of ease.
With a wave of her tentacle, laughter peals bright,
'Life underwater is pure dynamite!'

So here she swirls, bold and unbound,
In the embrace of the waves, joy is found.
In her gelatinous form, freedom sings clear,
The sea's celestial drifter, spreading cheer!

Journey to the Heart of the Ocean

Bouncing on the sea's bright floor,
A squishy blob, it starts to soar.
With tentacles that flail and sway,
It giggles as it drifts away.

With a flip and a flop, it makes a splash,
In a dance that's kookie and full of bash.
It whispers jokes to passing fish,
Seeking friendship with every swish.

Catching seaweed in a friendly race,
Wobbling with remarkable grace.
"Oh, look at me!" it shouts with glee,
A floppy hero of the sea!

Sailing past a crabs' crabby frown,
It tickles octopuses, spins them 'round.
With laughter echoed through the foam,
This jiggly creature makes the sea its home.

Embraced by the Currents

A wobbly blob in the sea's embrace,
Twisting and turning, it knows its place.
With giggles bubbling like a seaweed stew,
It rides the waves, till it's all askew.

"Hold on tight!" the current laughs,
As jelly bobs like silly drafts.
With each crest and each dip, it plays the fool,
Making waves in the sea's grand pool.

Meandering past a shark with surprise,
Who can't help but blink his big, wide eyes.
"Oh be careful!" he rumbles, full of dread,
While jelly just wiggles its squishy head.

The ocean's jester, so carefree and bright,
Winking at fish, a comical sight.
Dancing through bubbles and swirling cheer,
A merry traveler with nothing to fear.

A Dance of Grace

In the blues and greens, a sight to behold,
A jelly draping like a shimmering gold.
With twirls and spirals, it captures the sun,
An artist afloat, just having fun.

Wiggling like a noodle in a cooking pot,
It floats along, giving laughter a shot.
"What a life!" it hosts a bubbly affair,
As fish clap flippers, all stripped of care.

Spinning in circles, it's dizzy with joy,
A jiggly dancer, no need for a ploy.
It takes a bow to the cool ocean breeze,
While dolphins burst out, cheering with ease.

Chasing after shadows, a playful game,
Each poke and prodding just adds to the fame.
With elegance, grace, and giggles so loud,
This jelly contorts, a slippery cloud.

Whispering Waves

The waves are whispering, soft as a sigh,
While jelly floats gently, saying hi.
With a wink and a wiggle, it spins through the spray,
Making jellyfish secrets, in a cheerful ballet.

"Oh look at me!" echoes through the blue,
A jiggly wobbler, with a grand view.
It bumps into crabs who just shake their claws,
While laughing at fish and their silly jaws.

With a twirl and a swirl, it flaps like a kite,
Challenging currents to join in the flight.
Underneath coral, it tickles the reef,
Causing a ripple of merry disbelief.

The ocean giggles and bubbles with glee,
As jelly dances, wild and free.
With each wave that kisses the golden sand,
The jester of the sea makes a splash so grand.

An Enigmatic Glide

In a sea of blue, oh what a sight,
A wobbly blob takes off in flight.
With tentacles flapping, a dance in the tide,
It twirls and it swirls, with nothing to hide.

A giggle erupts from a curious child,
As the creature wobbles, a bit too wild.
'Is it a jelly, or is it a sack?'
It drifts with a grin, and laughs right back.

Floating along, with no need for speed,
It munches on plankton, a gelatinous feed.
But oh the confusion, is it here or there?
Dancing on waves, with jellyfish flair!

As bubbles arise, the fun fills the air,
This silly sea thing has no word to spare.
With a jig and a shake, it slips out of view,
A giggling whisper, the ocean rings true!

Abyssal Secrets

In depths mysterious, where sunlight fades,
A wiggle with secrets in midnight parades.
With a bell-shaped hat and a ruffled cloak,
It's the prankster of waters, oh what a bloke!

It sneaks up on crabs, gives them quite a scare,
'What was that bump?', they wiggle in despair.
With a bubbly chuckle, it glides out of sight,
'Just a wobbly buddy, don't give me a fright!'

Coral crew tries to keep it inside,
'Stay in your lane!' but the jiggler won't bide.
It's got jokes to tell, a tale to unfold,
In a swirl of the sea, it's the jest in the cold.

So if you find giggles beneath the waves,
Know it's the jelly, with all that it braves.
A trickster by nature, free-spirited cheer,
In the realm of the deep, it embodies all here!

Interlude of Light

Oh glimmering glider, you sparkle and shine,
With oceanic grace, an enigmatic vine.
Flitting through currents like a spark in the sea,
A dance so delightful, so wild and so free.

With each gentle sway, it tickles the waves,
Eliciting laughter from all that it braves.
A light in the gloom, a whimsical glow,
What magic lies there, where few dare to go?

Pulsing like lanterns, a glow in the night,
Swirling and twirling, such a marvelous sight.
It plays peek-a-boo with the flickering rays,
As sunlight beams down to add to the praise.

So here's to the jiggle, the jig, and the gig,
The rhythm of water, so joyful and big.
In the depth of the sea, where the laughter runs deep,
Is the creature of jest that we all want to keep!

Celestial Drifter

In the ocean's vastness, like stars on the floor,
Wobbles a traveler, seeking for more.
With a jumble of colors, it glitters and glows,
'The night's just begun!' say the creatures down low.

It flops with a giggle, a slap and a splash,
Dancing through currents, in a whimsical dash.
With a jiggly jig and a humble old grin,
It knows all the secrets where laughter begins.

Each swish brings the fun, a ripple of cheer,
Floating like dreams, it drifts without fear.
A cosmic ballet, a celestial ride,
In galaxies blue, it's the joy of the tide!

So raise up your voices, to the whims of the sea,
For the jester within that's forever so free.
In funny adventures beneath waves divine,
Is the drifter of laughter, the jiggler in line!

Ocean's Embrace

In a world of bubbles and salty spray,
A gooey creature floats, come what may.
With tentacles wiggling, a dance so wild,
The ocean chuckles at this jelly child.

Bobbing along in a dreamy sway,
It greets crabs and fish on its playful way.
With a wiggle and jiggle, it catches the eye,
Spreading giggles, oh my, oh my!

When it catches a wave, what a funny sight,
A squishy balloon in the morning light.
It sprays some water, as if to say,
"Join my circus, let's splash today!"

Oh, what a lark in the briny blue,
With jelly pals, this crew's never through.
Under the sun, like a carnival ride,
In ocean's embrace, they gleefully glide.

the Silent Ambassador

A floaty diplomat with no need for words,
It waves to the fish, those swift little birds.
Paddling through currents with grace and charm,
This globby envoy brings laughs, not alarm.

With a wink from a tentacle, it grins so sly,
"Who needs a suit when you can just fly?"
Holding no meetings, just soft ocean breeze,
It mingles with seaweed, tickles the knees.

"Let's organize chaos!" it seems to declare,
As it tumbles and rolls, without a care.
Bouncing around with a giggle and flip,
This ambassador says, "Join my trip!"

In a match of the waves, it leads the charge,
With blobby excitement, it feels quite large.
Swaying to music that only it hears,
Bringing giggles and joy, brightening fears.

Glimmers of a Coastal Nomad

In the sunlit splash, it floats on by,
A traveler lost, oh, where will it try?
With bio-luminescence, it plays like a star,
Illuminating paths to adventure afar.

Through rocky beaches and sandy shores,
It answers the wave's call with friendly roars.
Sprinkling sparks as it glides with ease,
This roaming delight dances in the breeze.

"Where to next?" it asks the crabs in line,
"Perhaps a salad? Or some ocean wine?"
With bubble trails leading, it swirls and twirls,
Charming the ocean, making friends in whirls.

No map in hand, just a curious mind,
With every new wave, it leaves all behind.
A lighthearted wanderer, full of glee,
In glimmers of joy, it hearts the sea.

Swaying in the Rhythm of the Waves

With a jig and a jog through the frothy spray,
Our jelly friend dances, come what may.
Swaying and gliding to nature's own tune,
Bouncing to beats beneath the bright moon.

It throws a party for sea grass and shrimp,
"C'mon, my friends! Let's have a blimp!"
With each bob-and-weave, it gently sways,
Finding the fun in its wobbling ways.

"Here's a jelly jig, come join my refrain!"
It laughs as it twirls through the salty rain.
No worries today, just a show of delight,
As it dances through fading, fading light.

In the bubbles we see, reflections of cheer,
As the rhythm of waves holds our hearts near.
With every splash, our spirits do soar,
Swaying with laughter, forevermore!

A Chronicle of Marionette Dreams

In the depths of dreams where the currents weave,
A jelly puppet dances, oh, what a spree!
With strings made of seaweed, it twirls and whirls,
Creating a saga of flips and swirls.

With every flopping tug, it paints the sea,
As shrimps in tuxedos cheer gleefully.
"Look at me, I'm a star!" it proudly proclaims,
As the ocean applauds with bubbling frames.

Marionette mischief, it flirts and it plays,
Inventing new tales with zany arrays.
Tangled up in laughter, it tries to break free,
With bravado and charm, in its watery spree.

Each wave is a stage, and the light is a friend,
As this jelly performer twists 'round the bend.
With every leap, it finds joy in the tides,
In a world where fun and mischief abides.

Timeless Voyage

In a bubble of jelly, here I go,
Drifting through waves, moving slow.
With a jiggly dance, I float and sway,
Hoping a fish won't take me away.

I wave to the crabs as I pass by,
They look so grumpy, oh my my!
With a twist and a turn, I twirl around,
I hear the ocean's funny sound.

Duck diving dolphins, oh what a sight,
They laugh and leap, such pure delight.
I wave my tentacles, doing my best,
They grin and shout, 'Want to join our quest?'

Through whirlpools and eddies, I glide with glee,
Playing tag with a seaweed tree.
Oops, got tangled, what a goofy mess,
But I giggle, what fun; I must confess!

Veils of the Ocean

In sparkling waters, I slip and slide,
Like a silly ghost on a tide's wild ride.
With a body so squishy, floating along,
I bumble through bubbles, singing a song.

I peek at the turtles, they roll their eyes,
While I curve and twist with joyful cries.
Are they judging my dance? Oh, what a shame!
They just don't get my jellyfish game!

A starfish applauds with its arms spread wide,
Cheering for me as I glide and glide.
I try a new move, a spin and a flip,
Oh wait, I forgot, I am supposed to drift!

Those fish with the fins, they sure are snappy,
With tails that swish, so bright and zappy.
I laugh, they just stare; it's quite a charade,
But deep down they know, it's a fun escapade!

Cresting Hues

Upon the crest of the wave, I play,
Waving to boats, 'Come join my ballet!'
With colors so bright, oh what a sight,
I giggle and shimmer, pure delight.

A seagull swoops down, what a rude shock,
I bounce and I wiggle, like a jelly clock.
He squawks in surprise as I twist in the air,
'You're not a snack, I promise, I swear!'

The seaweed tickles, what can I say?
Like tickling fingers in a giant buffet.
While fish swim by with a curious glance,
I throw out my tentacles, come join my dance!

The sun begins setting, a glowing array,
I bob in the colors, a slipstream cliché.
What a delightful end to my silly day,
In the midst of the ocean, I joyously sway!

Caress of the Current

Oh, what a whirl with the tide I spin,
With a giggle and jiggle, let the fun begin!
As the current caresses, I laugh with delight,
Bobbing and weaving, oh what a flight!

My friends, the cuttlefish, paint the scene,
They change colors fast—so sleek and keen.
I wave my tendrils, 'Catch me if you can!'
But they roll their eyes; it's a humorous plan!

A playful seahorse drifts by my side,
He makes funny faces, we laugh with pride.
'We're the goofballs of the blue!' I declare,
Together we frolic, without a care.

As the bubbles rise up, towards the light,
We twist and we turn, what a joyful sight!
With a flip and a flop, we bid goodnight,
In our bubbly ocean, everything feels right!

Celestial Wanderer

In the ocean, with a wobbly sway,
A bobbing blob dances day by day.
With tentacles flapping, a floppy show,
It's the goofiest traveler, don't you know?

Floating freely near the coral reef,
It tickles fish, causing them grief.
"Oh, what a sight!" the sea stars cry,
As the jellyfish glides, oh me, oh my!

With a cheeky grin, it spins around,
Splashing colors wherever it's found.
Each dip and swirl, a clumsy feat,
This jelly knows how to bring the beat!

As the sun sets, it glows so bright,
A jelly disco, quite the sight!
Under the waves, it twirls with glee,
A jovial jester, wild and free.

Ghostly Currents

In murky depths, a wraith-like wave,
Floats a jelly, stylish and brave.
With a transparent jig, it starts to twirl,
Scaring fish with its ghostly swirl!

"Boo!" it shouts with a jelly giggle,
As schools of minnows start to wiggle.
With every pulse, it makes a scene,
A haunting presence, but it's not mean!

Chasing bubbles, it takes a break,
Puffing up like a soft, squishy cake.
With a wink and a jiggle, it's on parade,
In a spooky ocean masquerade.

As night falls, it lights up the sea,
A ghostly glow, so fancy and free.
Jelly shenanigans under the moon,
A whimsical dance, a watery tune.

Luminescent Odyssey

Glowing bright in the depths so deep,
A jelly slides without a peep.
With iridescent flair, it takes the stage,
In a sparkling show, it's all the rage!

From coral caverns to sandy bays,
It wobbles and jiggles in comical ways.
"Look at me!" it gleefully shouts,
As crabs start clapping with their front clouts!

A luminescent flair, it's quite the sight,
Bouncing around like a kite in flight.
With every gleam, it spreads some cheer,
A glowing jelly, spreading joy here!

When tides are high, it rides the wave,
A playful spirit that's ever so brave.
In the oceanic ballet, it steals the show,
With its glowing charm, we all feel the glow!

Whispers of the Tides

In moonlit waves, soft whispers flow,
A jelly floats with a gentle glow.
It gabs with shrimp, giggles with eels,
Sharing secrets that the ocean feels!

With a squishy laugh, it swirls around,
Spreading joy in the underwater ground.
"Have you heard?" it teases with glee,
"Flounders are fancy, just look and see!"

Chasing seaweed, a playful race,
It slips and slides, a whimsical chase.
With each tidal pull, it dances along,
Singing silly tunes, a jellyfish song!

In the watery depths, it finds its friends,
A merry crew, where laughter never ends.
So if you glimpse this sneaky delight,
Join the fun in the ocean's light!

Secrets Beneath the Surface

Bubbles giggle in the tide,
Nudging friends, they take a ride.
Tentacles tickle, a jolly dance,
Swirling round in a glimmering trance.

Under waves, they spread the cheer,
Whispers of fish say, 'Come over here!'
A flick of a fin, then a splashy grin,
Secret shenanigans, let the fun begin!

With a swish and a sway, they twirl and spin,
Tales of the ocean echo from within.
The crusty old crabs watch with a frown,
As these floaty clowns flip upside down!

So if you're feeling blue and down,
Join the jellies in their frolic town.
In the deep, where giggles thrive,
There's a party waiting, come dive, come dive!

Seraph of the Sea

In a gown of translucent grace,
Swirling softly through space.
With a wink and a jiggle, it flies,
Leaving fish with big, round eyes.

It floats past the coral, oh so spry,
Waving hello to a passing fry.
'Hey there, finned friends! Care for a laugh?'
They giggle and wiggle, all on a path!

With each jolt and each bounce, they stir the tide,
Creating mischief, with nothing to hide.
A splash of seaweed flutters around,
'Join our parade, let joy abound!'

So come watch this seraph do the twist,
In the ocean's ball, you won't want to miss!
Underneath the winking stars,
This heavenly jester plays, oh so bizarre!

Ethereal Drifter

Dancing through the salty brine,
With jelly-like moves, so divine.
A curious glance, what's that up ahead?
An octopus chuckles, 'Oh come, be fed!'

With a bounce and a flick, it wobbles along,
Tagging along to a silly song.
A crab with a cap joins in the spree,
Kicking up sand like a dance party!

The waves swirl around in their happy shouts,
While sardines giggle, bursting out doubts.
'Are you a driftwood, or just having fun?'
'I'm a dancing delight under the sun!'

So float along with the feel of the sea,
Each wave a laugh, just let it be!
In the ocean's embrace, where joy swims free,
An ethereal drifter, as happy as can be!

Navigating the Briny Deep

Through twilight tides, they make their way,
Wobbling onwards, come what may.
With jelly smiles bright against the blue,
Daring each whirlpool to swallow them too!

Seven sea snails applaud their grace,
One snail exclaims, 'What a wild race!'
Tentacles waving, the jellies cheer,
'Let's dive and twirl, we've nothing to fear!'

Beneath the waves, silly games abound,
Chasing bubbles, what joy they've found!
A playful dolphin joins the throng,
Together they sing a splashy song.

So if you hear laughter in the deep,
It's jellies frolicking, their secrets to keep.
With seaweed and bubbles, they skip and glide,
Navigating the ocean with giggles and pride!

Glimmering Trails

In the deep sea dance of glimmers,
A wobbly blob does nonchalantly swim.
With a tangle of arms that wiggle and flail,
It's a jelly-shaped joke in a glittery gale.

A fellow fish looked on with a grin,
"Are you lost, my friend, or just on a whim?"
The jelly just bobbed with a wobble so grand,
"I'm on an adventure, care to lend a hand?"

They set off together, quite the strange pair,
One gliding smoothly, the other with flair.
Each wobbly flap sent the fish in a spin,
While jelly laughed loud—oh, what a fin!

Through coral jungles and kelp forests green,
They jived through the currents, a sight to be seen.
With each little giggle, they floated along,
A duo of joy, singing jelly-like songs.

Tentacles of Time

With flair in the fluid, a polka-dot glow,
A jellyfish travels with nowhere to go.
Its tentacles tickle the time with a jest,
"I'm late for a date!" it proclaimed with zest.

Soon it bumped into a clam, all in shock,
"You can't rush art, it's more like a clock!"
The jelly just floated, all yelps and delights,
"You're right, dear friend, let's just enjoy sights!"

Through bubbles and ripples, the minutes they'd twirl,
As a curtain of seaweed began to unfurl.
"Tick tock, let's play hopscotch in brine!"
It sashayed, it shimmied—a dance so divine!

Now the clam just chuckled, what a sight to behold,
With a jelly that wiggled, quite brave and bold.
"Who needs a schedule? We've plenty of time,
In a world full of giggles and oceanic rhyme!"

Fluid Starlight

In the twilight shimmer, with bobbles all bright,
A jelly drifts by, a whimsical sight.
With arms in the water, it looks like a star,
"Join me! Let's twirl—I've come from afar!"

Wrapped in the currents, it takes to the sky,
"Do you dare, little fish? Let's fly, oh my!"
The fish just giggled, and wobbled in place,
"I can't fly, silly! I'm stuck in this space!"

"Then let's make the waves dance, just you and me!"
"What fun it would be, oh come, can't you see?"
So they wiggled and rolled in a watery show,
Each twirl and each flip a spectacular glow.

With laughter like bubbles, they conquered the night,
Stars in the sea, everything felt just right.
As friends in this ballet, with bubbles they spun,
Who needs the skies when the dance has begun!

Beneath the Veil of Water

Under waves of azure, a comical sprite,
With a bell-shaped body and tentacles bright.
"I'm a squishy balloon on a playful spree,
Watch me bounce, watch me pop—what a sight to see!"

It wobbles through gardens of glowing sea grass,
As fishes all giggle, they wiggle and pass.
"What's that? A jelly? Oh look, it can spin!
With flutters so funny, you gotta come in!"

With a flick of its arms, it pretends to take flight,
Chasing after bubbles, all giggly delight.
The octopus chuckled, "You think you can race?
But I've got eight legs, baby, pick up the pace!"

Yet the jelly just laughed, an unruly facade,
"One, two, three, four, come on, let's applaud!"
They tangoed and twirled, all under the deep,
A spectacle of joy, so vibrant, so sweet!

Ethereal Wanderer of the Deep

In a cloak of wet and wavy grace,
Drifting without a care or pace.
Wobbly friends dance in the tide,
Each a goofy guide to the ride.

Oh look, a crab with a puzzled stare,
As jelly wobbles round with flair.
Tentacles waving, what a sight!
Floating free, a silly fright!

Fish are giggling, bubbles burst,
In this sea of laughs, I'm immersed.
Who knew the ocean could be so bright,
With jelly daydreams and aquatic light?

Bouncing off rocks, a comical sight,
Chasing seaweed with all my might.
In this realm of laughter and glee,
I'm the jelly making waves so free!

A Tidal Tale in Transparency

Once a curious blob in the tide,
With a bounce and a jig, I glide.
Flashing my colors, a funny show,
As the fish all laugh and throw.

A sea horse chuckles, 'What's up with you?'
I respond, 'Just trying out something new!'
With silly spins and wobbly dips,
I charm my way past finned tight-lips.

Barnacles snicker stuck to a wall,
While I twirl and take a fall.
"Life's a dance!" I bubble in glee,
As waves carry me so carefree.

With each gentle sway, laughter swells,
In every bubble, a story tells.
Floating along where the giggles play,
I'm the ocean's own ballet!

Luminescent Secrets of the Sea

Under the waves, I shimmer bright,
A glowing bulb in the deep, the light.
Who knew these tentacles could tease,
As I wiggle and jiggle with ease?

The clownfish chuckles, "What's that glow?"
I respond, "Just a light-up show!"
With a flash and a splash, I take the lead,
Bouncing along, oh what a deed!

Swimming past kelp with a gigglish flair,
Wobbling around like I haven't a care.
Catching the eyes of a curious eel,
Together we dance, what a surreal reel!

When sea turtles sigh, "What's going on?"
I bubble with laughter at rising dawn.
In this glowing splash of joyful delight,
The ocean's secrets dance in the night!

Floating through the Blue Abyss

In the vast deep blue, I float and sway,
A jelly in motion, happy and gay.
With squiggly moves and a twisty glide,
The ocean's a playground, oh what a ride!

Anemones giggle, playing coy,
While I bounce around like a buoy.
Puffs of laughter bubble up high,
As I drift by with a squishy sigh.

Creatures peek out from the coral maze,
I send them laughter through my translucent haze.
With every pulse, I spread my cheer,
Floating and jiving, I have no fear.

Dolphins leap and join my dance,
In this aqua party, we spin and prance.
Embracing the fun in the ocean's expanse,
We're the funny ones, taking a chance!

Dance of the Ocean Spirits

In the blue they sway with glee,
Tentacles tickle, wild and free.
Bubbles burst with giggly sound,
While they twist and spin around.

A waltz of squishy, carefree bliss,
Each ripple brings a jelly kiss.
They giggle as the waves collide,
In a dance, they glide and slide.

With friends in tow, they swirl and twirl,
A sight to make the seabed whirl.
Nudging fish with silly pride,
In this bubbly, joyful ride.

And as the sun begins to sink,
They pause to splash, and then they wink.
In loops and loops, they take a bow,
An ocean show, oh, wow, oh wow!

Ethereal Voyage

Floating high on currents bright,
Jelly wonders, what a sight!
Caught in a swirling, salty draft,
In laughter, they drift and craft.

With moonlit beams to light their way,
They dance the night, a grand ballet.
Giggling softly, they take flight,
Chasing shadows, quick as light.

In underwater fancy dress,
They tease the fish with silliness.
A flip, a flop, a grin so wide,
In their gel-filled world, they glide.

As morning breaks, they sing and sway,
New adventures greet the day.
With seaweed hats and jelly crowns,
They roam around, no time for frowns.

Diaphanous Sojourn

A sea parade of jellies bright,
Wobbling given sheer delight.
With gentle waves, they softly glide,
On nature's stage, they won't hide.

They bob and weave, a playful spree,
In the briny deep, they're wild and free.
Squirty, flirty, moving fast,
Carrying giggles on currents vast.

Winking at fish with cheeky charm,
They swoosh and swirl without alarm.
Tangled in laughter with every flip,
On this aquatic, jelly trip.

And when they tire from all the fun,
They rest beneath a warming sun.
But dream of tales from days of yore,
In the deep blue sea, forevermore.

A Soft Embrace in the Depths

In gentle waves, they twirl and tease,
Like cotton candy on a breeze.
Cuddling close in ocean's swell,
Whispers of joy, they weave and tell.

With arms outspread, they wave goodnight,
To fish that giggle in delight.
Their silken dance, so light and bright,
Turns ocean depths into pure light.

Swaying slowly, they share a laugh,
Drawing circles as they chirp and chaff.
They prance through seas with bubbling cheer,
Spreading smiles to all who near.

As currents carry them along,
Their jelly hearts sing soft and strong.
Each wiggle and glide, a burst of mirth,
In the ocean's cradle, they find their worth.

Tides of Transformation

In a sea of jelly, oh so bright,
A wobbly dance, quite a sight!
Tentacles flail, quite a mess,
Who's leading who? I can't guess!

Riding waves like they're a ride,
Bouncing left, then quick to hide!
With each swell, they giggle and play,
Oh, what fun to drift away!

Sway of Serenity

Floating around like a big, soft hat,
Bobbing and weaving, just like that!
A gentle sway, a bubbly grin,
Who knew the ocean could be such a spin?

Sunlight glimmers, a dance with glee,
A wobbly tune, just wait and see!
Gliding through currents, with pure delight,
It's jelly-fun from morning to night!

Melodies in the Deep

Underwater tunes that tickle your ears,
Bubbles bursting, oh what cheer!
Jelly folks jamming, it's quite the band,
A concert of wobbles, unplanned yet grand!

With a plop and a swish, they shake and jive,
A symphony of giggles, keeping alive!
Listen closely, hear their quirk,
Ocean's melody, that's how they work!

Unseen Pathways

Drifting along on an ocean road,
Each twist and turn, an unruly code!
Where'll we end? Who's to say?
Navigation is just jelly play!

Through seaweed jungles, over coral caves,
With laughter and wiggles, oh how it paves!
A map made of waves, so fine and free,
Join the jellies, come dance with me!

Rhythms of the Azul

In the ocean's dance, they wiggle with glee,
Floating like bubbles, so wild and free.
A bounce here, a jig there, they twirl with style,
Swaying through currents, all with a smile.

With tentacles jumbled, they're quite the sight,
Tickling each fish, causing giggles of fright.
They shimmer like stars in a watery ball,
Gliding through blue, feeling ten feet tall.

A flip and a flop, they wave hello,
To crabs on the sand putting on a show.
The seaweed whispers, wanting to play,
With jellies who bubble and bounce all day.

Together they laugh, a quirky parade,
In a world where the dull simply can't invade.
The rhythms of azul, a party so grand,
With jelly-like joy, they boogie unplanned.

Flowing Through Echoes

Drifting through seaweed, they float with flair,
Making strange shapes in the ocean air.
With squishy wee bodies that jiggle and sway,
Little comedians, come out to play!

Echoes of laughter ripple through foam,
As they leap and they glide, far away from home.
They'll tickle a turtle, a cheeky delight,
In a deep salty world, it's a laugh every night.

Through currents and eddies, they sneak and they slide,
With giggles and wiggles, they take us for a ride.
Mimicking dolphins, they try to impress,
These jellyfish pranksters cause utter distress!

Oh, to be jelly, so light and absurd,
Floating through echoes without a care heard.
A slapstick affair, in the blue they beam,
In a comedy ocean—how sweetly they scheme!

Soft Murmurs of the Abyss

In the shadowy depths, a whispering jest,
Jellies are dancing, feeling quite blessed.
With each gentle pulse, they wiggle and tease,
Making the fish giggle, just as they please.

Their bellies are round, they bob like a dream,
A soothing sensation, like soft ice cream.
They pop and they swirl with a colorful glow,
Spreading laughter like waves as they sway to and fro.

In dark watery corners, they plot and they plot,
Members of the jesters' undersea hotshot.
With sparkles and wiggles, they have a fine time,
Turning the abyss into a laughable rhyme.

They float with the confidence of royal decree,
In their jellyfish kingdom, the coolest, you see.
With murmurs and chuckles, in depths they reside,
Soft giggles and glee in the dark, oh, how they glide!

Dreamscape of the Deep

In the deep-water realm, where dreams come alive,
Jellies play games, they jump and they dive.
With a bounce and a twirl, they shimmy through blue,
Painting the ocean in a magical hue.

They float like balloons, with colors so bright,
Playing peek-a-boo in the moon's silver light.
With tentacles trailing, they giggle and glide,
Creating a carnival, an underwater ride.

In currents they twirl, a slippery waltz,
Provoking a chuckle, they spin and they vault.
With joy in each pulse, they sparkle with cheer,
Making the deep sea a land of no fear.

So come join the fun, let your worries all flee,
Among jellyfish revelers, wild and carefree.
In a dreamscape of deep, where laughter takes flight,
With jellies so playful, it's pure, pure delight!

Echoes of a Drifting Soul

In ocean's embrace, a creature glides,
With tentacles waving, and no need for rides.
It dances on currents, no maps in sight,
Seeking the snacks in the moon's soft light.

With each wobbly sway, it giggles with glee,
Dodging the fish that just won't agree.
Its friends are the bubbles, they shimmer and pop,
In a world full of plankton, it never will stop.

A sunbeam is caught, oh what a delight,
Reflecting a disco of colors so bright.
As waves tickle gently, it swirls with a grin,
A wiggly wanderer, just living to spin.

No anchor to hold it, just laughter and flow,
What else can it do but just go with the show?
In solitude bliss, it floats with a cheer,
Echoes of joy, the sea's laugh in the rear.

In Search of the Moonlit Tide

A shimmer of light, beneath silvery waves,
Our gelatinous friend in a dance, it behaves.
With glimmers of jelly, it mimics the stars,
On a quest for the tide where the laughter is ours.

It bounces on ripples, a slippery sight,
Chasing shadows of fish that just aren't polite.
"Oh wait up, dear shrimp, don't swim out of view!
I come with these dances, alright, we'll debut!"

With a flick of its arms and a plop in the sea,
It twirls like a ballerina, full of glee.
Giggles ensue as it floats here and there,
A party of plankton joins in on the dare.

From dusk till the dawn, in its jiggly style,
This life of a drifter is perfect, no trial.
A comet of color, it sails through the night,
In search of a tide full of friends and delight.

The Fluid Odyssey of Silence

In a world made of water, it silently glides,
With jiggly appendages swaying like tides.
Much too fine for small talk, it whispers with grace,
An elegant dancer in a blue-water space.

Oh, who coined the term 'beware of the sting'?
This critter prefers just to laugh and to sing.
It floats with the fishes, without any shame,
Saying, "Hope you enjoy my translucent fame!"

Enveloped in solitude, yet never alone,
In a zany parade made of jelly and foam.
Taking life as it comes, with each wobble and sway,
The quest for good times in bubbles at play.

As the currents keep singing their jovial song,
The fluid odyssey simply can't go wrong.
With laughter like sea breeze, the journey's a blast,
In a world full of wonders, it's happy to last.

Translucent Tides of Existence

With soft purple hues floating in the deep,
A jellyly wonder that'll never lose leap.
Stirred by the tides that swirl and collide,
How perfectly silly is a jellyfish ride!

It jingles and jangles, a bubbly delight,
Making friends with the seaweed, all through the night.
"Hey, shrimp, come join me, let's twirl in a loop,
A party awaits in this seaweed soup!"

In patches of sunlight, it gleams like a gem,
The humor in jiggling, its own little hymn.
As bubbles rise up, it gives them a wink,
"Come ride on my waves, let's play and not think!"

Translucent and light, like a dream in a dream,
It flips and it flops with a giggle and gleam.
Such joy in the rhythm of water's embrace,
A jiggling existence, oh what a face!